BEASTLY BEASTS

John McLay

Illustrated by
Martin Brown

Orion
Children's Books

ORION CHILDREN'S BOOKS

First published in Great Britain in 2016
by Hodder and Stoughton

1 3 5 7 9 10 8 6 4 2

A CIP catalogue record for this book
is available from the British Library.

ISBN 978 1 4440 1599 7

Printed and bound in China

The paper and board used in this book are from well-managed forests
and other responsible sources.

Orion Children's Books
An imprint of
Hachette Children's Group
Part of Hodder and Stoughton
Carmelite House
50 Victoria Embankment
London EC4Y 0DZ

An Hachette UK Company
www.hachette.co.uk
www.hachettechildrens.co.uk

*To Louise Cripps and all of the children
and staff at Swainswick School*

Contents

1.
True or False?

Some creatures are real.
They might be big and scary
but they definitely exist.

If you look very carefully in the jungles of the world, or up in the skies, or under the sea, you'll be able to see them.

Other creatures, equally amazing, might exist. There have been stories about these beasts for hundreds of years.

A few sightings now and then, a blurred photograph, or a missing sheep or goat.

MISSING SHEEP

We like to hope these bizarre monsters are real.

Some animals are not real. There is no scientific evidence that they have ever existed.

No fossils.

No photographs.

These are the most amazing creatures of all.
We know about them from ancient stories
called myths and legends.

Storytellers (and mums and dads) have told tales about them for thousands of years.

They are huge. Colourful. Magic.
Dangerous. Brilliant. Beastly!

2.
Legends Around the World

The most famous beast around the world is the dragon. Dragons have bat-like wings and lizard legs and can breathe fire.

They appear in ancient stories and star in lots of books and films.

In England, in the Middle Ages, knights were
sent to slay a dragon.

Some had better luck that others.

In China, dragons are often shown as very colourful and very long.

In their time, the Vikings would have dragon heads carved into their boats to scare enemies away.

Some legends are told in only one country. In Tibet, there are tales of a big, hairy creature called the Yeti or Abominable Snowman.

Nobody has captured one yet and strange footprints are the only evidence that it might exist.

The American version of the Yeti legend is known as Bigfoot or Sasquatch. There is a famous photograph from 1967 – but experts think this is really just a man in a gorilla costume!

3.
Sea Monsters

Not all brilliant beasts live on the land.
Some are famous for being terrors of the sea.

Sailors used to tell stories of a monstrous sea creature called a kraken that was a bit like a giant squid.

It would rise up out of the ocean and use its
tentacles to sink a whole ship.

Everyone has heard of the Loch Ness Monster. It is said to be an underwater dinosaur that lives in modern day Scotland.

But is it real?
Could it live secretly, without being seen,
for so many years?

Several expeditions have tried to find the monster. So far, it has not been spotted. But people will never give up looking for it. Just in case!

Fish can be freaky, so it's not surprising that sailors used to think that some of them were real monsters.

Have you ever seen a frilled shark?
It has a long body, big eyes, three
hundred teeth and frilly gills that make
it look a lot like a sea serpent.
Very scary. Very real.

4.

Dangerous Skies

There is no hiding place from deadly, mythical creatures. Some creatures of legend could be found in the sky.

Dragons were said to fly using their big, scaly wings.

They could turn people into toast with
their fiery breath.

You would need to duck if a pterosaur flew over your head. Winged lizard-like dinosaurs from millions of years ago, they had long jaws and teeth like needles.

Watch out for the phoenix!

This very, very old bird could live for hundreds of years. Then, it would build a nest and set it on fire.

After the old phoenix died,
a new phoenix would
appear from the flames.

5.
Mythical Monsters

There are many strange creatures in the Greek and Roman myths from two thousand years ago.

Medusa looked like a woman but had poisonous snakes on her head.

Warriors who looked at her directly
were turned into stone.

Luckily, a hero called Perseus came along.
He defeated her by looking at her reflection
in a polished shield.

A creature that was half man and half horse was called a centaur.
In modern stories, centaurs are described as friendly but powerful creatures.

Cerberus was a three-headed dog who guarded the gates to the Underworld.

Cyclops was a massive one-eyed giant that stomped around bashing in old Greeks.

The Minotaur lived in the labyrinth of King Minos. It was half man, half bull, and always very hungry.

Mythical animals are all weird
and wonderful.

6.
The Truth is Out There

Some real creatures, living today,
are just as amazing and crazy as
the beasts of myths and legend.

Crocodiles can be mean. And deadly!

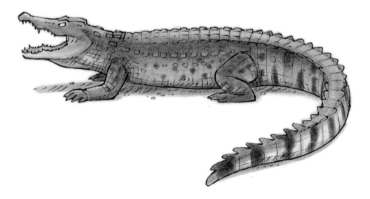

Some people believe they inspired
the dragon myths.

Narwhals have a huge tusk on their heads.
They are called the unicorns of the sea.

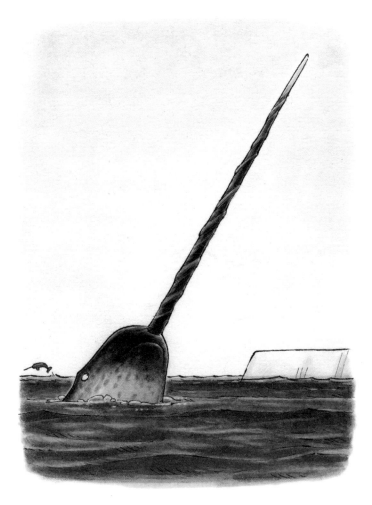

Do you have any idea how
big a blue whale is?

Heavier than a kraken and longer than a sea serpent, it can grow up to 30 metres long and weigh 180 tonnes. That's huge.

You don't need to look very far
in the real world to find amazing animals
and beastly beasts.

They might even be the same
animals that sparked the stories
of myths and legends.
Now that's amazing.

BEASTLY BEASTS

QUIZ

**Turn the page to test
what you can remember ...**

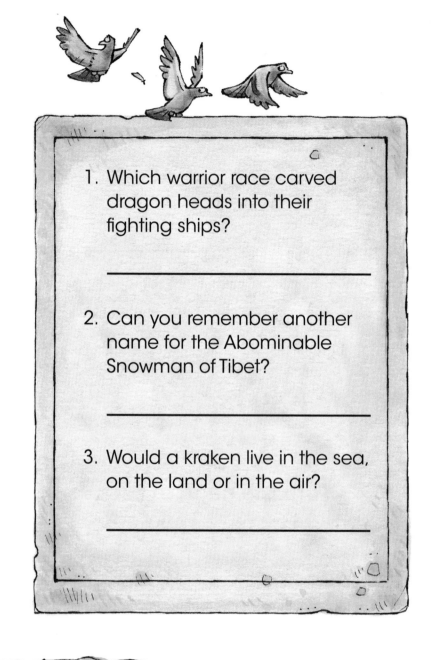

1. Which warrior race carved dragon heads into their fighting ships?

_____

2. Can you remember another name for the Abominable Snowman of Tibet?

_____

3. Would a kraken live in the sea, on the land or in the air?

_____

4. Which ancient bird set its own nest on fire?

_____

5. What animal did Medusa have on her head?

_____

6. How many legs would a centaur have?

_____

WHICH BEASTS DO THESE BELONG TO?

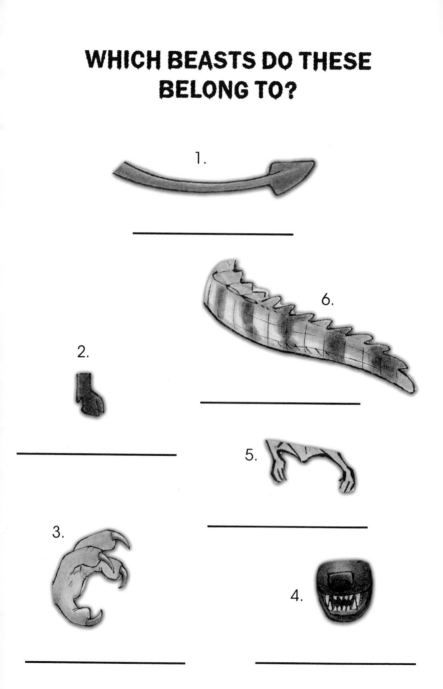

1.

_____

6.

2.

_____

5.

_____

3.

4.

_____   _____

7. _____

12.

8.

_____

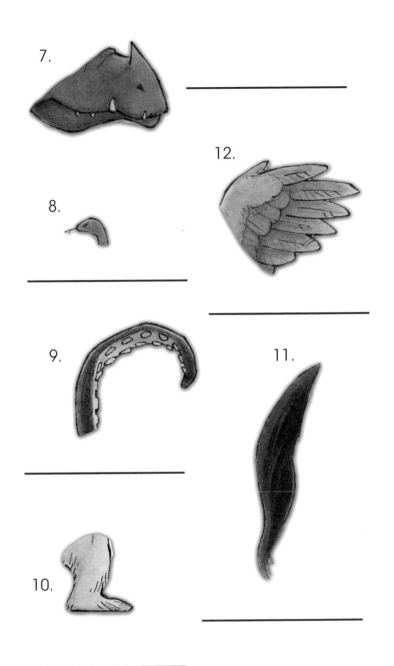

_____

9.

11.

_____

10.

_____

ANSWERS:

Beastly Beasts Quiz

1. The Vikings
2. The Yeti
3. The sea
4. The phoenix
5. Poisonous snakes
6. 4

Which beasts do these belong to?

1. Dragon
2. The Minotaur
3. Dragon
4. Cerberus
5. Pterosaur
6. Crocodile
7. Dragon
8. Medusa
9. Kraken
10. Yeti or Abominable Snowman
11. Centaur
12. Phoenix